"I Love Music - Anytime, Anywhere!"

I Love Music - Anytime, Anywhere! © Copyright 2003 by Rozanne de Fossard

Illustrations © Copyright 2003 by Peej

A catalogue record of this book is available from the British Library

First Edition: November 2003

ISBN: 1-84375-049-X

To order additional copies of this book please visit:
http://www.upso.co.uk/rozannedefossard

Published by: UPSO Ltd
5 Stirling Road, Castleham Business Park,
St Leonards-on-Sea, East Sussex TN38 9NW UK
Tel: 01424 853349 Fax: 0870 191 3991
Email: info@upso.co.uk   Web: http://www.upso.co.uk

"I Love Music - Anytime, Anywhere!"

Genuine and entertaining musical anecdotes

Compiled by
Rozanne de Fossard

Illustrations by
Peej

UPSO

Foreword

Humour has always been an important part of my life and equally so in my teaching. I simply could not have survived so many years of class music, choir and piano lessons without it! It has indeed been a natural and essential ingredient to a successful career and I would like to think it has kept me relatively sane over the years!

The combination of music and humour was bound to emerge sooner or later, as the inspiration for a collection such as this evolved from a life-time's experiences, appreciation and love of music.

In compiling this book and collecting material over the years from music teachers and from children, mostly between the ages of 5-15, I fully realise that I have only scratched the surface in this subject.

Music is clearly a powerful phenomenon. It has a considerable impact on the lives of so many people, young and old, whether instruments are played or music just listened to. "I love music - anytime, anywhere!" celebrates the innocence of children and their experiences with music, with some delightfully amusing comments as well as some pretty profound observations!

My sincere thanks go to all the like-minded music teachers from far and wide who not only were able to remember their amusing stories, but also generously contributed them to make this book possible.

I would also like to praise the superb illustrative work by Peej, who is the creator of the popular and ever imaginative music teacher, Miss Hayward! (See website.)

Grateful thanks also go to Val Smith, for her computer expertise; to David Pafford, Jo Lindsay and Sarah Murphy for their advice; to David Crabtree for his positive 'verdict' and to Victoria (Osborne) Reeve, for her unending support and encouragement.

This book is dedicated to the late and legendary South African teacher and concert pianist, Laura Searle, with whom I had the privilege to study and whose wicked sense of humour and inspiration well and truly left their mark!

Contents

"Music is a secret language" (Charlotte)

What is Music?

It's a form of art expressed in sound... (Matthew)

*...which is organised and normally sounds beautiful!
(Elizabeth)*

*It can be made by a machine which is made by man and
sometimes it makes a nice noise and sometimes not! (Tom)*

*Music makes different sounds and strange sounds too!
(Amelia)*

It is sound coming from singing instruments... (Runy)

...even your own voice is an instrument! (Alice)

*Music is a string of notes put together to make a tune...
(Alysha)*

*...so that the tune, rhythm and beat are all composed into
one. (Joe)*

*You line up the symbols so that you can read them to bang,
blow, hit or wallop your instrument! (Georgie)*

It's beats and sounds put together for entertainment. (Josh)

*Music is a hobby. It's written down in Italian. It's ancient
and it's good fun the more experienced you get! (James)*

*It's an activity that you do in your free time. It's a pleasant
source of enjoyment. (Alex)*

...and it's something that is a lot of fun! (Anon)

"What do you understand by a dot after a note?"

Chapter 1

Anecdotes

Individual lessons

"You hold it for 2 seconds longer!"

(Kate)

One of my pupils said he wanted to play the "Trumpet Voluntraly" (i.e. Voluntary). I couldn't resist replying, "Good, because I wouldn't want to force you!"

....

I had a slightly autistic pupil and I was trying to explain the Aural Test C, which is about recognising a rhythmic difference. The key chord was played and then the first note and before I could continue, the child eagerly yelled "That was different!"

(Graham Lewis)

....

My Grade 5 oboe pupil declared seriously, two weeks before her exam, that, having failed her Grade 4 scales because she hadn't given herself enough practice time, she was going to start straight away and wasn't ever going to let that happen again...Sigh!

(Philip Gittings)

....

A young pupil of mine played "Tarantella" faster and faster and when he'd finished, he beamed at me and said, "Did you notice I moved into turbo power?!" I couldn't help noticing his *molto accelerando!*

....

A little girl asked, half way through her lesson, "Do you know what, Mrs Carpenter?" "No, what?" I replied. "I hate piano!" came a disappointing answer!

....

I asked an 8 year old to name the key signature of D major. "Father Christmas!" came an enthusiastic reply!

....

A little girl of 6 years old told me that her Mummy and Daddy said they wanted her to learn to play the piano because it was better than going to football club. Well, I thought, at least I'm being useful somewhere!

....

One of my 7 year old pupils asked me at the start of our weekly lesson, "Do you know what my Mummy says about my piano lessons?" "No," I replied, intrigued to know the answer! "She says she's fed up having to do Chester Puzzles every week!" Now that shed some light on his written work, which had been a lot better than his practical lately!

....

MISS HAYWARD BEGAN TO WONDER WHETHER SHE HAD BEEN ENFORCING THE 'NEVER STOP WHILST SIGHT-READING' RULE A LITTLE TOO RIGOROUSLY...

9 year old Letisha had worked very hard to ensure she was getting well into the 'eyes on the music' and 'fingers on the keys' routine. She proudly informed me after playing her piece, "I can do it now! I used PVC glue to stick my fingers on to the keys each time I practised so that they didn't keep flying away!" I was horrified, but it had worked!

....

Questions that leave me *molto agitato:*
 - "What's the flat in G major? I did practise it!"
 - "What note's that?" Answer: "5th finger."
 - And "No I didn't practise it *that* way. Mummy said it should go *this* way..."

....

On my way to collect a lazy pupil who was late for her lesson, I met her coming up the stairs with her friend. She looked surprised to see me and then said, rather cheekily, "Why didn't you come and fetch me sooner? We thought you were lying dead behind the piano!" What morbid imagination and I thought to myself, "Yes and I'll bet you haven't practised again, have you?!"

....

I was telling a colleague of mine in the staffroom about a pupil who was doing well, venturing into a range of notes not used before, to which she replied, "Oh yes, just like Star Trek!"

....

A ten year old pupil was quite a musical chap, but was a great deal more successful with his sporting achievements. One lesson, he said to me, "I don't have time to practise because of my swimming and tennis commitments which I have to do, but my dad says I also have to do my Grade 3 exam this term..." (Oh dear, not again!)

....

During a session on aural with one of my Grade 1 pupils on Test C (recognising change) she replied that the rhythmic change had been in the middle, because the note in the middle had got half a beat louder!

....

After explaining what was meant by 'time signature,' I asked my young pupil Clara if she had understood. "Yes," she quickly replied, "and you're looking very pale today!" She is the daughter of a doctor.

....

I was surprised to read in a pupil's notebook, a note from an enthusiastic parent, who asked, after just 4 lessons, "When will Harry sit his Grade 1 exam?"

....

Rebecca was proud to show me how well she had practised "Little Santa" that week. She did, of course mean "Little Sonata!"

....

I try to instil the importance of counting a steady beat in, to set the tempo before starting to play a piece of music. One of my pupils counted in a steady beat "1-2-3-4," but then added "Ready, steady, GO" and off she went at break-neck speed!

....

After a careful explanation to my 6 year old pupil, Owain, about all the things he had to think about when playing his piece, I then asked him to tell me what he had to think about. After a pause, he said, "My brother's having his tonsils out today." Well, I suppose that was what was really important and certainly all he was going to think about that day!

....

I explained and demonstrated quavers to a young pupil of mine and then asked if he had understood what I had said. "Yes," he replied, very quickly, "and do you know that the ferries sail from Southampton?"

....

Six year old Abigail clearly did not like using her left hand at all. Being right handed, she remained adamant that her left hand did not work properly, like her right hand. Her father patiently sat with her through her homework that week and wrote a note saying, "We have persevered, but have not been very successful with the left hand this week. If this is what she's going to be like learning to use her left hand, I shudder to think what she'll be like learning to drive!" The image sprung to mind quite vividly!

....

We were discussing the lines and spaces of the staves and I duly pointed out that the spaces in the treble clef spelt 'FACE'. I asked Jeremy (8) if he recognised the word and, after some careful thought, he said "Fackey!" I burst out laughing and he very quickly corrected himself and said "Oh no! Face!" He became very good at recognising his spaces after that!

....

I was working on the 'Humpty Dumpty' (dotted quaver, semiquaver) rhythm with a 10 year old and he seemed to be getting the idea in a descending passage in 'Star Wars.' Suddenly, the passage collapsed and he lost it. "Oh, whoops!" he said straight away. "Humpty Dumpty had a great fall!" Brilliant and quick thinking, I thought!

....

My rather reluctant 9 year old pupil, Rosie, said to me one lesson, "I don't really want to play the piano any more. I'd rather play with the frogs in my friend's pond." Lessons were stopped soon afterwards - the frogs had won and what competition was I?

....

My 11 year old pupil Thomas always did his piano practice in the mornings before school. One day, his much younger sister, Naomi, had a great 'practice' on the piano and when asked to stop, by Mum, so that Thomas could do his practice, she replied, "It's OK, Mummy, I've done Thomas's practice for him!"

....

....

A 9 year old and very serious Grade 1 pupil played her entire first piece in her exam an octave lower. When she had finished, I asked her if she had realised this and she replied, "Oh yes, but I thought I'd carry on just in case the examiner didn't notice!" He must have, but she had stuck to the 'keep going' rule and came out of it with a merit!

....

I asked Roberta (a Year 7 pupil) what a tonic triad was. Even though we had talked about it before, to my utter dismay, she replied, "Sounds like something we learnt in chemistry!" Some of them just never listen!

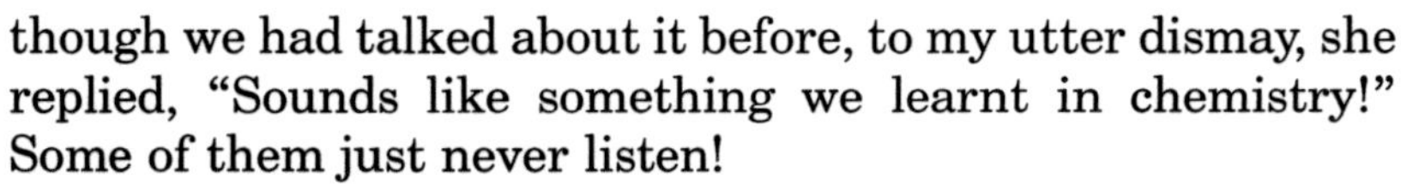

A musical 11 year old pupil was very interested to hear that most pieces finish in the 'home key,' so that the piece sounds 'finished.' "What a good idea to do that," she said. "Do composers do that on purpose?"

I was reminding a 10 year old pupil about accidentals in 'Darth Vader'. Pointing to an A flat in a bar, I said to him, "Remember the rule! How long does an accidental last?" I expected him to answer that it lasts for the rest of the bar, instead, after a long pause, he said, "Two beats!"

I suggested to Abigail that she might like to try some of the other pieces in 'Roundabout,' for extra reading practice as I didn't want her to get bored in the run up to her Preparatory Test. She quickly replied that she had already tried one, but gave up because Daddy had said she had played "exactly all the wrong notes, all the way through!"

I was explaining the Preparatory Test listening games to a young child and said I was going to play a short piece of music and she would have to tell me if it was loud or soft. Before I had a chance to play anything at all, she enthusiastically yelled out "It's loud!"

I demonstrated the Grade 1 C major scale in contrary motion to 8 year old Myles and only played one octave, as required.

He immediately exclaimed "But Miss, you only played one verse! There are supposed to be two verses!" I'd been unaware that he'd gone on and learnt two octaves (verses) on his own!

....

OCCASIONALLY, MISS HAYWARD WISHED SHE'D NEVER HIT UPON THE 'ACTIVE INTERPRETATION' IDEA...

....

Six year old Tamara appeared to understand that the first seven letters of the alphabet are used to name the white keys. "Oh yes", she said, "D for Denham (her surname), E for my friend Ella, but," she paused, "where's T for Tamara?"

....

A young Grade 1 pupil looked very puzzled and turned to me

saying, "I really don't understand why they haven't invented an E major scale yet!"

....

Eight year old Jeremy, who was a very musical child, was very excited one day when he suddenly exclaimed, at his lesson, without any prompting, that he realised what he was doing when he read music. He said, with great delight, "I'm decoding the notes - I can make this page come alive!" True and what perception!

....

A colleague came into my teaching room inbetween lessons, looking absolutely exasperated. "That's it", she said, "I know what it's all about. 'We' cannot count in 3 - only 2 or 4. 'We' are anti-rhythm!" I knew exactly how she felt!

....

A very talented musician and colleague is known for his, perhaps, occasional lack of patience with his not-so-talented pupils. Apparently, one day he was seen fleeing from his teaching room into the corridor for a 'breather,' covering his face, shouting "Nurse! Nurse!"

....

Eleven year old Sarah walked into her Grade 2 viola exam clutching her instrument and music. She was surprised when the rather jovial examiner greeted her by saying, "Good morning! What have we here - a trumpet?" She said afterwards that she had felt immediately relaxed. (What a good tactic, I thought!)

....

After listening to an 8 year old play through a short piece and knowing what a struggle it had been, I wanted to encourage

Six year old Isabelle was curious to know what the quavers were at the back of her first piano book. I gave her a brief explanation, as she wasn't quite ready for them and then pointed out that I happened to be wearing a brooch with two quavers beamed together. She looked at them and then at me and said "You've got two 'd's' joined together on your brooch!"

her and said, "Well done, Anna, that was very nice." But before I could go on, she replied, "My teacher says that 'nice' is a boring word!" Sometimes, it's difficult to find a suitable adjective, but I've been careful not to use that word since!

....

Six year old Clara astounded me when, after a short and simple discussion about different kinds of pianos, she looked at me and said, "Mrs Carpenter, did they have pianos in the olden days when you were a little girl?"

....

A ten year old boy was attempting to learn the James Bond theme from "Dr No," but he was having a little difficulty with the rhythm. After a lengthy explanation of what I thought should suffice, I tried to get him to 'say' the rhythm to help - i.e. 1&er,2&,(3)&,4& etc. He agreed quite confidently saying, "OK, I see - din-diddle-in-di*n*-din-din-din!" Well, he'd got it and clearly the 'din-diddles' were far more exciting than plain, boring old counting! We didn't have a problem after that!

....

I was recently explaining to a 10 year old pupil the meaning of the word 'triad,' in preparation for her Grade 1 broken chords. I have to be very clear with what I say, as there have been times when she has completely misunderstood an instruction. I thought it would be perfectly straight forward, when I asked her to look at the 'tri' in the words 'triangle' and 'tricycle' and then ask herself what she thought the 'tri' meant. She replied, "To do your best!"

....

Eight year old Richard was enjoying Part 2 of a well known piano tutor book. One of the pieces near the beginning has the right hand playing a chord of 2 semibreves or just a single

The piano I had to use in a school had a seriously out-of-tune F sharp. My young pupil couldn't wait to show me a special piece introducing F sharp. He proudly performed it, not noticing the F sharp and was rather amused when I said, "Thank you," and very quickly added, "we won't play in that octave until the piano tuner has been!" I brought his attention to the out-of-tune key and playfully put my hands over my ears. "I can't stand it!" I said. Then, to my utter dismay, he stood there and deliberately and repeatedly played the F sharp with a very naughty look on his face, watching my agony. It was a torture to my ears and he was enjoying every second! I finally managed to convince him this was not a good idea and please would he stop doing that and leave the key alone! Reluctantly he agreed and I'll never forget his name - Damien!

note semibreve, throughout the whole piece. When we turned to look at it for the first time, he said to me, "What are all these number eights doing all over the page?" I suppose the semibreve chords did look like number 8s!

....

I was accompanying 11 year Emma on the piano while she played her clarinet. We were practising 'O, when the saints' and she always found the rests quite tricky. At one stage, she didn't count them at all and when I stopped to point them out to her (as tactfully as I possibly could) she answered back, "I did stop at the rests. I had a rest and then I carried on!"

....

9 year old Sophie amused me when we were discussing famous composers. She asked, "Wasn't Beethoven the one who cut off his ear?"

(Rozanne Carpenter)

....

On a Grade 5 theory paper, a pupil said that S.A.T.B. meant "Start At The Beginning."

(Tamsin Bird)

....

A young pupil of mine was having difficulty with a short phrase containing an acciaccatura. As many times as I played it, he repeated it, leaving out the acciaccatura. Becoming a little exasperated, I asked why he would not play the little note. He replied "Because it's crossed out!"

(Mrs M. Jeffrey)

....

"Do you know why people want to play the violin, Meredith?"

I gave several suggestions in reply. Her reply was "No! It's because when you're big you can play really fastly!"

(Elizabeth Dwinnell)

....

Whilst preparing minor scales for an examination, I said to Simon, "You aren't really getting the hang of these melodic minors, are you? Anybody would think they were called moronic minors!"

(Ann Armstrong)

....

Question: "If the spaces are F A C E, which is the second one?"
Answer from a 7 year old boy, "D."
Oh dear...

....

Having suggested to Andrew that he ask his mother to call out the letter names so that he could 'hop the octave,' this 6 year old replied, "The trouble is, my mother can't help me because she thinks the piano goes from A-Z!"

....

After discussing treble and bass clefs, 7 year old Johnny placed both thumbs on Middle C and said, "Oh, I see. This is the border and the ones up here on the right are the light ones and these are the dark ones down here on the left!" Interesting!

....

This might sound familiar to a number of music teachers out there...
I have a very irritating and reluctant 8 year old pupil, who definitely does not want to come to his lessons, but is

Clifford was struggling with his piece in the usual rather laborious way, when all of a sudden, he gave a sharp intake of breath, winced and shot his hands off the keyboard. "Why Clifford, whatever's wrong?" he was asked. He replied, "Please, Sir, that note's cold!"

(David Carr)

unfortunately pushed into playing by his over enthusiastic mother. On various occasions, I have had to suffer comments like "I don't like rhythm" after many patient explanations and "I don't like the piano, in fact, I don't like any musical instruments at all!" Even worse was "Has the lesson finished yet?" and "I wish it was tomorrow." The last straw was "Well, how old are you, anyway?" He'll be learning with someone else next term!

(Margaret Chave)

....

My six year old pupil was confused with her left and right hands. Her reason for this was the high notes on her piano were in a different place - this was because the piano was on another wall!

(Kate Williams)

....

A theory pupil struggled with the concept of intervals: augmented 3rd became 'argumentive' 3rd!

(Liz Lane)

....

Thomas asked if he had to play his piece again, as his hands hurt. When asked "Why?" he replied, "Because I've been playing in the sand dunes in the half term holiday!"

(Anon)

....

My cheeky pupil said to me, "Please don't talk to me while I'm interrupting you!"

....

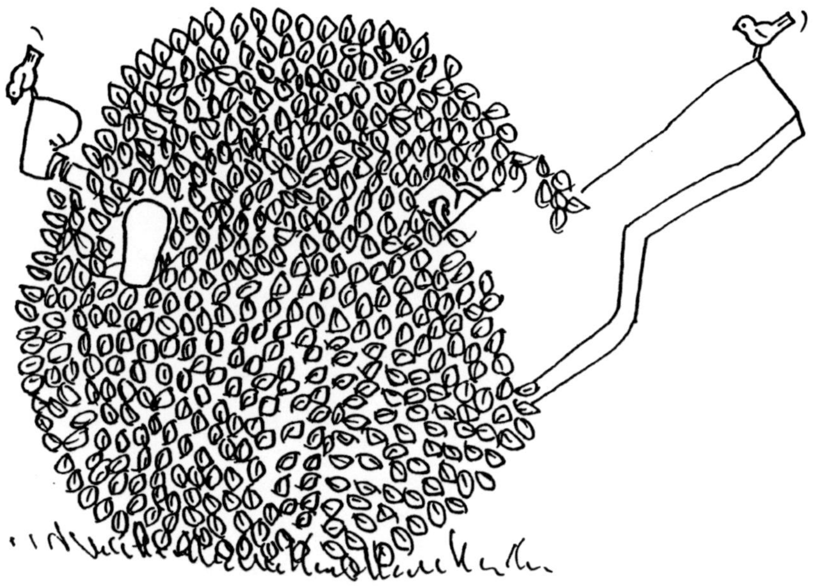

Katy walks home every week from her lesson, carrying her cello. She says that one day, the cello got blown into a bush by a strong wind and she was still holding it!

(Anon)

....

In a sight-reading session, the teacher asked "Haven't you forgotten something?" meaning the accidentals. The pupil replied "Oh yes, those mistake things - are they accidents?" Heard this one before?
A teacher said to her pupil "Put your finger on that note." So the pupil put his finger on the page!

....

Teacher of the double bass: "I'm having a dreadful time with this lot. They're still playing first fingers with their thumbs!"

....

After having a piece for a week, a pupil said -
"I've memorised it already and I can play it standing on one leg!"
I'm pleased to say this chap became 1st violinist in the National Youth Orchestra, so he must have 'both feet on the ground!'

(Susan Humphreys)

....

I told my 9 year old pupil, Mark, how Beethoven had composed, despite losing his hearing. The next lesson, he returned, having looked through a simple Ländler by Schubert. He told me confidently that Schubert must have also gone deaf, as the piece did not sound too good. On playing the piece to me, I discovered he had misread the bass clef for the treble clef! (No wonder!)

(Anna-Maria Raffa)

....

One child, when asked to complete two boxes with the sign for a sharp only filled in one. When asked "Why?" the reply was, "I only know one sharp!"

....

A small girl aged 9, always made a particular mistake and her teacher said, "that's your 'bête noire.'" "What's that?" the girl asked. The teacher explained. At the next lesson, the girl stumbled and said, "Oh, that's my boudoir!" It took the teacher seconds to realise what she had meant!

(Mrs M.A. Hobbs)

....

Joan had been having piano lessons for a whole term and her progress was very slow. One week, I asked her how often she practised and she replied, "When I go to Granny's." "Have

I had a very keen 8 year old pupil who, just prior to her Grade 1, broke her arm. Although she was not supposed to play her clarinet for several weeks, her father was so keen for her to take the exam, he decided to 'risk her arm.' I took her into the exam to accompany her and carefully lifted her arm out of the sling. The examiner said "Oh dear!" My pupil looked at her very seriously with large blue eyes and replied, "My daddy says if I don't pass, he'll break my other arm!" I'm pleased to say she achieved a distinction!

(Lynne Sharratt)

you been to Granny's this week?" I asked. "Oh no", she said, "Granny lives in Guernsey!"

....

Christopher was taking his Preparatory Test and although a little nervous, went in, fully prepared. When he came out, I asked him how it went. "OK," he replied, "but Middle C wasn't in the same place as on my piano!"

(Rachael Sims)

....

Playing many wrong notes in a piece, a pupil stated, "This piano is not in tune. Can I tune it, please?"

(Anon)

....

7 year old Robert proudly declared, "I'm going to play the theme from Dvořák's New World Sympathy!"

(Hilary Brooks)

....

I had just given a detailed explanation about a very difficult passage on the violin and the pupil responded by coming up rather close to me and saying, in a very quiet voice, "Excuse me, Sir, I think you've missed a bit above your top lip this morning!" Not exactly the response I was looking for!

....

I was complaining that the music shop had mistakenly charged me £110 for four G strings (for the violin), when a colleague, who just happened to be passing by, very quickly quipped, "Are they diamond studded? You can get then much cheaper at Ann Summers!"

(Richard Crabtree)

....

I explained to a pupil how to quickly identify the spaces in the treble clef by using the word FACE and to use the rhyme 'All Cows Eat Grass' for the spaces in the bass clef. The following week, he still could not remember the bass clef spaces and so I asked him to think about the rhyme about what the cows do. The child excitedly replied "All cows make noise!" He quickly realised his mistake and we laughed. The most favoured words seem to be 'All Cannibals Eat Grannies!'

(Victoria Reeve)

....

....

After an individual lesson at home, Alex's mother said, "I'm really pleased - he's beginning to enjoy the piano now, after 4 years and he's beginning to practise by himself now!" At last! I must have been on the right track!

....

After giving 4 lessons to a beginner pianist, I was rather surprised when the mother asked me when I would be dealing with phrasing!

....

I had just returned from a stint of examining and I explained to a pupil what I had been doing. He said that I did not look like an examiner and I asked him what he thought they should look like. He replied that all examiners looked grumpy!

(David Hobourn)

....

A pupil on crutches was physically escorted to the lesson by her parent, so that she wouldn't miss a lesson. Does this give a new meaning to the word 'keen'?!

(Anon)

....

I explained to a young beginner that we use the first 7 letters of the alphabet to name the white keys and duly demonstrated. She looked at her fingers and then at me and said, with a very puzzled look, "But Miss, how do I play seven keys? I've only got five fingers!"

(Ethel-Jane Cormack)

....

My wife Gaynor, who is a teacher of the piano, gave a very young pupil a sheet of theory questions, one of which required the notes to be named. They surely were. The child gleefully handed in her work a week later, with the notes having been given the names of every child in her class!

(Peter Barnes)

....

Giving an 8am lesson to a 5 year old was never my best time. One morning, I said something that was quite nonsensical. When apologising to the pupil, I used the excuse, "Sorry, I'm still asleep!" Little Amos looked at me in total amazement and said, "But your eyes are wide open!"

....

Having prided myself on holding little Oliver's attention as I played a short piece on my violin, he demonstrated his rapt attention with the remark, "Did you know that hair grows out of little holes in your head?"

....

I was giving an adult a lesson one day, on how to change position on the violin, using a guiding finger. Having observed my careful demonstration, she said, accusingly, "Isn't that cheating?"

....

A pupil, aged 4, was excessively fidgety in her violin lesson. After putting up with this for quite sometime, I said, "Oh do stop messing about, Hannah-May! It's so boring!" Quick as a wink, she quipped, "Not for me!"

....

Being a bright 4 year old, Hannah-May was never short of a return. Wanting her to speak up louder in answer to a question, I pretended that I was hard of hearing as I was so 'very, very, very old.' She looked at me with large brown eyes and said brightly, "I'm still new!"

....

A very earnest father of a violin student in the Suzuki method, was having an attempt at playing his daughter's piece. His performance, given with great confidence, was so utterly appalling, that I was totally speechless! I could feel my jaw hanging open and, try as I might, not a word would come out. My silence rather surprised him, so after a moment or two, he said with a smile, "Shall I play it like that again?" With much effort, I was able to manage a very weak "No - not like that. Do something else!" (The laugh I had inside myself was the best yet!)

(Diana Dixon)

Rhoda, aged 14, had a quick, but quiet sense of humour. On playing a note out of tune, I called out "That's sharp!" She over-compensated on the correction, so I called out "That's flat!" She turned to me and said "Well, make up your mind!"

....

An over confident 16 year old was playing some fairly advanced repertoire, albeit carelessly. I had to draw her attention to numerous corrections and each one of my corrections met with an arrogant "I know." Finally, I snapped and said "Don't say that phrase again! If you weren't so slapdash, I wouldn't have to make so many comments."
A few moments later, while playing in the key of D major, she played a C natural, instead of a C sharp. On pointing this out to her I got in return, arched eye-brows and she said, in mock amazement, "Well now, I didn't know that!" I found her remark hilariously funny so we finished the lesson in a happy frame of mind.

....

Benedict, at the age of 4, asked if he could have a star at the end of the lesson. "Oh no", I said, "you don't get a star just by asking for one, it has to be a reward for a very good lesson and today's lesson wasn't really your best." The following week, he had a wonderful lesson and I was busily talking to his mother about how well it went and why I was so pleased. Little Benedict got my attention and then said carefully, "Diana, are you thinking of anything?"

....

I had mentioned the meaning of the words 'pitch' and 'rhythm' to 8 year old Michael. "Now", I said, "what do you think the word 'expression' means?" "I know", he said, "it's when you bash it!"

....

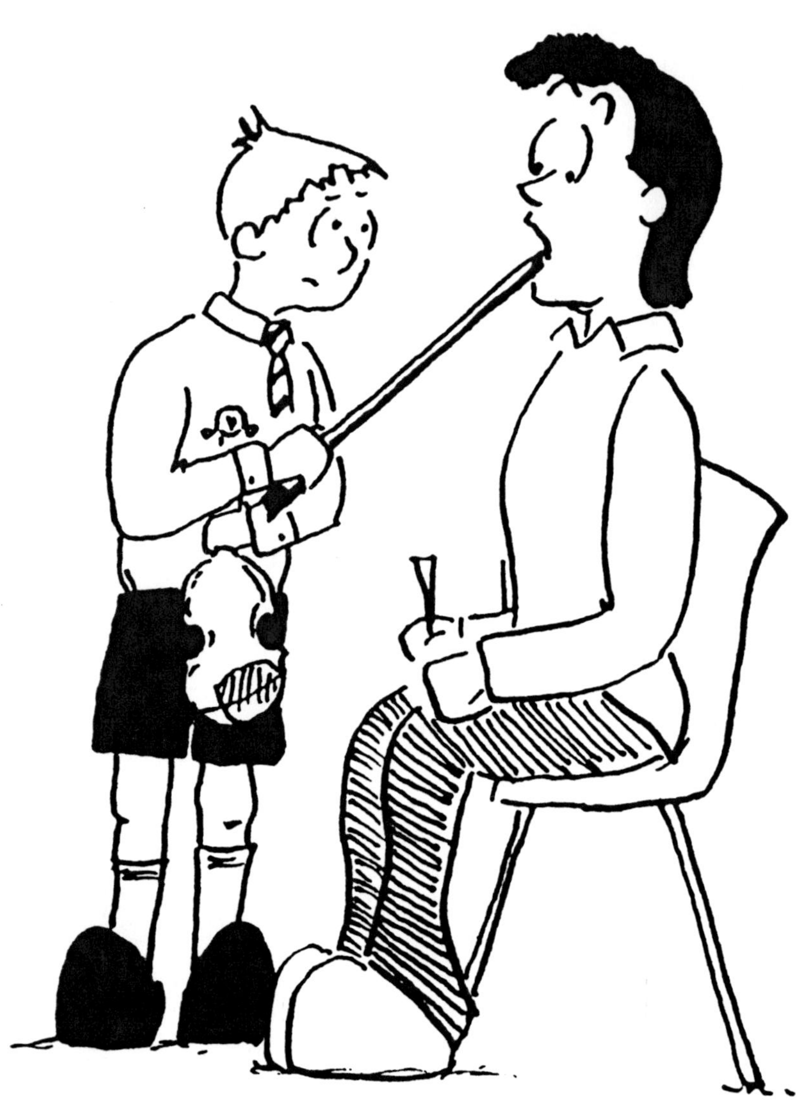

Sitting at eye level teaching Johnny, aged 5, in a violin lesson, he said something delightfully funny that made me guffaw. My laughter soon turned to embarrassment when he said, "Golly, haven't you got a lot of fillings?"

(Diana Dixon)

After giving a lesson to a young pupil, I said I was going to get on and do some practising of my own. The child replied, "I thought you knew all the notes by now!"

(Diana Dixon)

....

A friend of mine's 5 year old twins had been excited about the fact that they were going to learn the piano. A week after the first lesson, I saw them in the garden and said, "I hear you are learning to play the piano," to which one of them replied, "Oh no, we learnt that last week!"

(Anon)

....

Reason for being late for lesson:
"My fish was giving birth."
Apparently, mummy fish will eat the baby fish unless they are scooped out and put into a separate tank...

....

Teaching three 14/15 year olds 'Papageno's Song' set for the Grade 3, I wanted the last staccato as marked, so I asked them to do the last bar as follows:
"F - rest - F - off."
Needless to say, they fell about laughing!

(S.M. Rabson)

....

A foreign friend said to me, "So you teach music. Do you teach the piano?" "No," I replied, "only the cello." "Oh, you see," she went on, "I am looking for someone to teach my son to type..."

....

I had a 9 year old beginner cello pupil, who had also started having piano lessons and practised neither. One day, she said to me, "Mrs Russell, you will be glad to hear that I'm stopping the piano so that I can concentrate on the cello now. I've learnt all the notes on the piano, but I'm learning new notes on the cello every week!"

....

....

Cello teacher, after weekly nagging, "Sarah, why do you always play very sharp?" To which she replied, "Well, you see, I find it much more comfortable to have my hand further down."

(Philippa Russell)

....

After a slightly disappointing exam result, I tried to encourage a pupil by saying, "Never mind the result, try to look at the big picture and how well you've progressed generally..." To which the girl replied, "Oh, I don't mind. The examiner spat when she spoke and had halitosis!"

(Loraine Worley)

....

I have to smile when I remember asking one young boy if he'd practised 'Pop! Goes the Weasel' during the week. Quick as a flash he replied, "No, 'cos my mum hates weasels!"

....

When asked what the dynamics in a piece of music were, an enthusiastic reply was, "EXPLOSIVES!!" Very vivid, I thought!

(Anon)

....

An American candidate was being examined by a friend of mine and in the Aural Tests, was asked to recognise the time signature. "Six-eight," he replied. "Thank you", said the examiner, "now beat it." So the American left the room!

(Anon)

....

On discussing an exam result with a pupil who had achieved a merit, the 8 year old said, "I was hoping to do better, because my sister got an extinction!"

(Richard Eastham)

....

A little girl always started her pieces on the wrong note. Each lesson, corrections were made and by the next lesson, she would be starting on the wrong note again. One day, she came in and said, "I've discovered why I always start on the wrong note!" Apparently, on her keyboard at home, mum had tried to be helpful and put sticky labels on each key, telling the letter name - unfortunately, she had put the wrong letter names on the keys! (Familiar? Parental contribution!)

....

A dad, who's daughter had just begun to have piano lessons, looked at her music and was puzzled by the small numbers underneath each note. Seeing the numbers 12345 in the left hand going downwards and needing to learn the three notes below, he continued with 678! Imagine his surprise when he discovered the small numbers were actually fingerings!

(Anon)

....

I had an exceptionally talented young violin pupil who performed Elgar's 'Salut d'Amour' with great gusto and in completely the wrong style. When I asked him why he had performed the piece in such a military fashion, he said "Well of course I did. The title says 'salute the armour!' So I did!"

(Natalia Gittings)

....

A surprising excuse for missing a lesson:
"Sorry I didn't come to my lesson yesterday - my mum took me to lunch in Rome."

(Andy Hampton)

....

One of my husband's pupils turned up with a trombone slide firmly superglued in, as his dad thought it was loose!

(Ms M. Rusmanis)

....

An examination candidate announced that he was going to play "Because" and then "Minute!" (i.e. Berceuse and Minuet!)

(Jenny Tribe)

....

....

I got the usual very quick response from 7 year old Becky when I explained what a natural sign was. "Oh yes", she said, always ready with an answer, "there are two meanings to this word. One is to 'naturally have a baby,' and this one means 'to play the ordinary note,'" she concluded, in her very matter-of-a-fact manner!

(Anon)

....

After 6 year old Lewis had played 'Boating Lake' very badly, I said to him, "That went a bit wrong, didn't it, Lewis?" He replied "Yeah, it's the piano that was wrong. It's not very in tune, is it?"

....

A 6 year old was having problems following instructions. After explaining finger numbers at his third lesson, I asked him to put '3' on 'E'. So he put 3 fingers down on the 'E' all at once!

(Anon)

....

Seven year old Jessica was very amused by all the new words she was being introduced to. After hearing 'semibreve, minim and crotchet,' she laughed and said, "Oh! More gobbledegook!" When I told her about 'bars' she said, "Oh yes, these aren't the kind that you go and have a drink in, are they?"

(Anon)

Rhythm - everyone's favourite!

Rhythm is the organising of sounds in time. (Steph)

*It's something that makes sense to the music teacher!
(Georgie)*

...or it makes no sense at all! (Joseph)

Rhythm? It's that beaty thing, you know! (Owen)

I hate rhythm! (Sheridan)

....

Describing ornaments

An ornament is a decorative twiddle... (Claire)

...in music which makes it sound interesting. (Charlotte)

Isn't is something you put on your mantelpiece? (Rebecca)

I think it's an old object that's worth something... (Matty)

*It's a valued, treasured thing like a glass jar from the year
1020. (Rosie)*

Ornaments? Is it something fragile? (Charlotte)

....

A metronome is...

...a little man living in an inner city. (Anon)

If you don't have a conductor, a metronome keeps you in tune. (Jessica)

A metronome is an instrument that ticks like a clock...(James)

...and gets really annoying! (Katy)

I don't know why my metronome still works because I've thrown it around so much, it makes me very cross because it just doesn't tick with me! (Anon)

....

Majors and minors...

Major is higher, I think and I prefer it to minor because that's what my dad is in the army. (Harriet)

...it sounds happy with flats and a minor sounds sad, with sharps. (Andrew)

A major sound is bigger than a minor sound! (Oliver)

...it's loud, like me and a minor is normal. (Anita)

Major sounds jolly and a minor funereally. (Claire)

...it's nice, but minor is nasty, with too many flats! (Steph)

A minor is kind of Egyptian. (Luke)

...it sounds evil...(Jonathan)

...and frightening and scary...(Tansy)

...it's spooky! (Rosie)

....

mispronunciations...

skitarto (staccato) (Anon)

skitzo and shirtzo (scherzo) (Anon)

apaches and archipoligos (arpeggios) (Anon)

prestimetio (prestissimo) (Sheridan)

....

"I've not practised...

Chapter 2

Practising
and
excuses, excuses!

...mummy forgot to remind me!"

(Sue Libera)

Practising -
on the plus side...

....

....

It's good to practise because it stops my teacher having a wobbly with me! *(Lily)*

Practising is great, because I've got a great teacher! *(Anon)*

It's useful, because it can be an enjoyment, as well as getting a piece better! *(Gabrielle)*

I enjoy playing the drums and I like practising because it's fun just to play from your heart. *(Alex)*

I like practising because I feel really good when I can do something new! *(Krystyna)*

Practising is how to play an instrument and you can't play an instrument unless you practise! *(Edward)*

I play, but I don't get taught, so I practise whatever I want, whenever I want! *(Ed)*

Practising and Excuses, Excuses!

Practising is good because it puts you ahead to the next lesson. *(Ricky)*

...what has to be done, must be done. Good, because it makes you good... *(Graham)*

I think practising is good because you could become a famous pop, rock or rap star! *(Runy)*

It's a very good idea and I myself should do more! *(Luke)*

You need to practise if you want to get somewhere with your playing. *(Franny)*

I practise because my dog sings to my saxophone!
(Andy)

It's a task that must be done!! If you don't, then you'll never learn anything! *(Georgie)*

I love practising because I can hear improvement all the time! *(Sarah)*

When someone makes me practise, I don't want to, but when I get into it, I quite like it! *(Harriet)*

I think you need to practise and a little and often is better than a few big chunks! *(Andrew)*

It's fun, as long as you can have some play time! *(Tansy)*

My teacher gives me nice things to practise! *(Laura)*

It's good to practise because I think when you know what you're doing, it's much more fun. *(Hannah)*

...if you're bored, you can practise and also, your mum and dad will like to hear you. *(Blaire)*

It's important because it makes you remember it and you learn to play it properly! *(Kaye)*

You can learn a lot by practising and, as they say, 'practice makes perfect!' *(Shane)*

It's necessary and without it, you are useless! *(Sam)*

If you want to do well, then you must practise. *(Charlotte)*

....

...and on the down side...

I hardly ever practise because I can't find the time. *(Jamie)*

It could be scaled down a bit! *(George)*

It's hard, because I always forget the tune! *(Edie)*

I don't like practising! I don't think anyone does! *(Ashley)*

I play the piano and I think practising should be exterminated!!! *(William)*

It's OK, but it takes up too much of your time. *(Edward)*

I don't think much of practising! *(Chris)*

...it gets on your nerves after a while! *(Alex)*

I don't like music when I'm made to play! You have to be in the right mood! *(Hannah)*

I don't like practising the sax because you have to put it together every time! *(Emily)*

I must say, I hate practising! *(Paris)*

Practising is horrible, horrible, horrible horrible and MORE HORRIBLE! *(Danielle)*

We're not keen on practising! *(Charlotte and Emma)*

It's dull and my mum annoys me during the process! *(Anon)*

Practising is OK but sometimes I wish I was watching TV! *(Olivia)*

....

I was learning to play the recorder and I found practising quite hard because I had to learn the notes!

(Jade)

...it can be boring, because you have to get up from the television and get your instrument out and play boring pieces... *(Sophie)*

Piano is easy, because you can just sit down and play it, whereas the flute is such a hassle to get it out and then you have to clean it as well... *(Sarah)*

I get told off when I forget to practise! *(Emma)*

I think it's more of a chore! *(Nicola)*

...you have to be in the mood! *(Carine)*

It's OK, but not every night! *(Georgina)*

I like learning the piece and doing it for the teacher, but when he tells me I'm doing it wrong, I get annoyed! *(Abigail)*

I think practising is hard and do not think we should have to do it! *(Paul)*

....

...could it not be so bad after all?...

I don't really like practising - it's boring but necessary. *(Olly)*

It isn't fun, but it's worth it! *(Jen)*

You have to do it, or you won't get anywhere... *(Lindsay)*

It's absolutely boring, but it gives a good result! *(Marek)*

When it comes to practising, it depends how I feel. If I've had a bad, tiring day, with loads of homework, the last thing I want to do is to practise, but sometimes it helps! *(Clair)*

It makes you actually learn the piece, so you learn to live with it. *(Becky)*

Practising an instrument is a bit of a bore, but when you're on stage, you feel very excited! *(Andrew)*

When it comes to it, I hate doing it, but when I get to my lessons, I see that it was very good that mum makes me do 20 minutes a day! *(Rosie)*

I like hearing myself get better and better! *(Polly)*

Excuses, excuses!

....

A young pupil of mine said he couldn't practise because "There was a mouse in the upright and the 'gran' was in store!"

(David Hobourn)

....

I haven't had time to practise.
It sounded better at home.
I have a different edition.
The editing is awful!
I practised it faster.
I brought the wrong glasses.
These aren't my fingerings!
The page turn messed me up.
My nails are too long!
My bow needs new hair.
I didn't know we were repeating.
I have new strings.
I don't like the piece anyway!

(Joan Sidgreaves - a list of the most common excuses over the years!)

....

It was obvious that my 7 year old pupil had not done much practice that week and was very keen to give me his list of reasons, which went - "I've not practised because I think I need glasses because I can't see the music very well because the stool is too low and..." I stopped him just there and asked what his mother had said. "Oh, she thinks I'm making it all up," he replied. We haven't had a list of excuses again (and there's nothing wrong with his eyesight!)

....

Abby declared that she was not able to practise on Thursdays, as it was 'Pet Attention Day.'

....

Sasha arrived at her lesson without her books, yet again. Her excuse this time was that "Mummy was in a frightful tizz because the cleaner had put the lodger's trousers onto the wrong wash..." Needless to say, this rather lame excuse did not go down very well!

....

8 year old Abaigeal apologised that she had not done any practising that week because she had been unwell: "I think I must have that millennium bug - have you heard about it? It's going to spread all round the world!" I had to reply with the appropriate explanation!

....

Excuses from a devoted and dedicated father read in his daughter's notebook:
"This week's excuses for not having done any practice:
1 - Mummy is away
2 - Daddy busy with school play.
Well at least they're different from those before!"

....

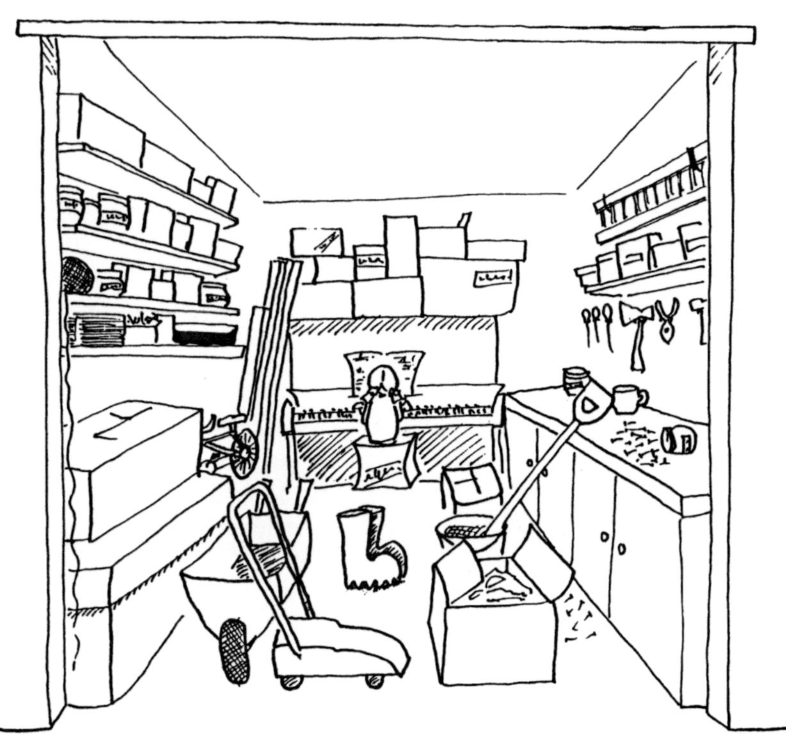

It's difficult to practise because the piano's in the garage!
(Anon)

I couldn't practise because mummy said she couldn't stand it anymore!

(Anon)

....

A young pupil of mine said he didn't know what he was supposed to have practised that week, because he didn't know where his books were and that "Mummy had probably vacuumed them up on Saturday, because that's all she does every Saturday!" (now there's imagination, I thought!)

....

I asked 7 year old Rhodri why he had not done his practice yet again. To my surprise, he replied, "I think you should know why I can't do my practice all the time!" Slightly taken aback, I said I didn't know why and asked what he meant. He went on to say, very sternly, "Well you should know by now, oh yes you do! We go to our Welsh cottage at the weekends!" "Well, that's all very well, but what about the rest of the week?" I asked. There wasn't an answer for that!

....

I couldn't practise because my pet rabbit had babies...
(Robert Andrews)

I can't practise because I don't have a piano and mummy says they're too expensive to buy anyway!
No, I don't have time to practise.
Practising interferes with my homework!
I prefer to roller-blade than do any practising.
I can't find my books anywhere. I think they must have slipped down behind the piano after my last lesson!
My little sister drew all over my books, so I couldn't practise!
Mummy wouldn't let me practise.
The dog chewed up my books...
So why do I have to practise anyway?

(Rozanne Carpenter)

....

I haven't been able to practise this week, because we don't in fact have a piano at home!

(Robert Andrews)

....

It was obvious that my 10 year old pupil hadn't done any practice during the holidays. When asked why, she replied, "I went riding and fell off my horse right onto my head and I completely forgot what you had asked me to do!"
I thought it was a brilliant answer and we had a good giggle.

(Wendy Partridge)

....

I couldn't practise because the dog was sick on my music.

(Anon)

....

Sorry, I couldn't practise, I fell down the stairs yesterday!
Sorry, I've not practised, it was my Nan's birthday.
I didn't practise the difficult pieces you gave me - I practised the ones I could play instead.
When asked for G major scale to be played, I said, "Have you

practised this one?" "Yes," was the reply. "What note does it start on?"

(Sue Libera)

....

A girl who obviously didn't want to practise her trumpet that week at all, went to the extraordinary lengths of burying it in the school rose garden! Needless to say, her prank didn't work, as when she said it had been stolen, it was discovered that she still had the keys and the case which was locked!

(Anon)

I was very surprised when two little girls, who were sisters, told me that daddy couldn't stand it when they practised their recorders. They had to go into the garage, get into the car, shut the doors and then they could practise! That way, he couldn't hear them!

(Lindsay Bowden)

....

Sadly, one of my pupils returned to school at the beginning of a new term, saying he was very sorry he was unable to practise over the holiday, as there had been a war and he and his family had had to leave the country and he no longer had his music books. It was perfectly true.

(Jenny Tribe)

....

Having collected a pupil two weeks running (who should have arrived on his own) and who once had no music with him as well, I asked him, in exasperation, "What's your excuse this week?" Silence. "My dad's depressed!" he replied.

(Anon)

....

A child did not have his books for his piano lesson because they were in such a rush that morning because the hamster was underneath the floorboards!

(Anon)

A foreign teenage guitarist, who clearly had no intention of practising his guitar, came to a lesson with bullet holes in his case and in the guitar itself! Apparently what had happened, was that he'd been doing his target practice in his bedroom and had propped his guitar case up behind bricks and books to protect it. Unfortunately, the shots managed to go straight through the bricks and books and consequently, the guitar itself was damaged! He was therefore quite unable to do any practice - whatsoever!!

(Anon)

Music is...

...An expressive musical language. (Nicola)

*It's like a story, but written with notes, rather than words.
(Emily)*

*...and you can express your feelings without having to use
speech! (Anon)*

*It's exciting because you want to know what's coming next!
(James)*

....

It's something that can change your mood. (James)

It can make people laugh, relax or become sad. (Lara)

*Music can calm you down or when you're down in the
dumps, it can make you happy again! (Isobel)*

It relieves stress. (Luke)

...it's a cool way of chilling. (Anon)

It can give you a special feeling...(Harriett)

...and bring back memories of a time or place. (Nicole)

Music is something that you both hear and feel. (Anna)

...you play the notes to express the feelings. (Charlotte)

...it can make all your troubles go away! (Alysha)

....

Music is something for all ages. (Georgia)

*...it's a pleasure that will be with you for the rest of your life!
(Chris)*

*Music is an ongoing mixture of sounds which sound nice or
nasty. If you play properly, you could make up nice tunes
which could be remembered for centuries! (Owen)*

*It's a luxury because some people in poorer countries
don't have good instruments... (Sabina)*

Music is useful to drown out my brothers! (Steph)

"I don't know why, but whenever I sing in class...

Chapter 3

Music at school

...everyone starts to laugh!"

(Claudia)

In my daughter's music class at school, the children were asked to give the Christian names of certain composers. On being asked about Verdi, she supplied the name of Monti!

(Mrs M. Jeffrey)

....

A class had been learning about instrumental families. When asked which member of the violin family played the lowest notes, the answer came back firmly - "the basement!"

(Mrs L. Mitchell)

....

In exploring ambience and sound stereo, a blindfolded girl was asked to point where the sound had come from. After a few completely wrong attempts, she then informed me she was as deaf as a post in one ear!

(Robert Harvey)

....

Answers given in a school music test:
1 - Agnus Dei was famous for her church music.
2 - Music sung by two people at the same time is called a duel.

(Anon)

....

Answers in a music exam:
The fog horn is a member of the brass family.
The sinballs are in the percussion family.
An oratorio is a bible story set to music and there is a lot of sinning in it.

(Sandra Maizels)

....

Teacher: What is the Italian term for 'at a walking pace?'
Student: Al dente. (Andante!)

(Andy Hampton)

....

10 year old Jane : "Can we go and play with the Casanova in the attic?" (clavinova!)

....

10 year old Susan: "The class have all gone to the rectal room." (recital room, i.e.!)

....

I was leaning on the piano during a class lesson and said facetiously, "I just don't know how music teachers used to stand up in the olden days before they had pianos to lean on!" Nine year old Fiona immediately said, "They leaned on harpsichords!"

....

9 year old Olivia took my breath away during the singing of "Farewell and Adieu to you Spanish Ladies." I explained that 'adieu' meant the same thing as 'farewell.' "Well", she said, "that's a tautology!"

....

Children write funny things in tests. 10 year old Hilary wrote about the violin: "The violin can be plucked or played."

....

11 year old Michelle was writing an essay during a cover lesson when I was absent. It was Christmas and the task was: "You are a missionary who has recently landed on a hitherto undiscovered tropical island and have just converted the natives to Christianity. Describe their first Carol Service." Michelle had the missionaries busy with preparations - photocopying carols for the natives!

....

At a boys comprehensive school where I was a peripatetic string teacher, at the first lesson, violins were sorted out and distributed amongst the children and the first lesson duly given. At the second lesson, one boy proudly produced his violin with a flourish - covered in deluxe white gloss paint, saying "Me mum said it was all scratched and old and it should have a nice new coat of paint!"

(Ms M. Rusmanis)

....

Perhaps one of my all time favourites was in February 1985. I decided to contribute to the tercentenary of Handel's birth by decorating the classroom with handles. There were door-handles, broom-handles, loo-handles, etc. Seven year old Emma entered and was puzzled. I started to explain.
"Have you heard of the composer Handel?" I asked.
"Of course", she said, "Handel and Gretel."

....

There was also the time in September when the 8 year olds were watching a recording of the "Last Night of the Proms." The camera panned across the promenaders in the front row.

I explained that they had been queuing for days in order to get their place in the front. "No wonder their beards are so long!" said Kirstie.

(David Williams)

....

Children are impressionable. Some years ago, we sang 'Jonah Man Jazz' just before the school exams. This unfortunately influenced the Religious Studies question on this topic, whereby Ninevah became 'a really groovy place' where everybody partied and enjoyed 'rock 'n roll all day long!'

(Robert Andrews)

....

Teacher: "Name the lines and spaces on the staff."
Child: "These are exactly the same notes as in my piano lessons!"

....

Teacher holding up a tambourine - "What do we call this instrument?"
An infant replied, "A tangerine!"

(P.J. Williams)

....

Playing a piece of music for the class to identify the number of beats per bar, a pupil, when asked "What time is it in?" replied "Nearly half past three!"

(Anon)

....

When asked what form the middle section of a movement was in, the answer was 'feudal.'

....

Answers from a class music test:
The trumpet sounds quieter because it has mutated (i.e. muted!)
As Beethoven was dead, he had to compose with his ear resting on the piano to feel the vibrations.

(S.M. Murphy)

....

Young William wrote:
The Quiristers are singing in Elgar's 'The Dream of Deuteronimus.'

(Hilary Brooks)

....

At St. Ursula's School, in a performance of Japanese drumming, the leader, who was dressed beautifully in the Japanese kimono, shoes and was made-up, etc., asked the children if they knew the most famous things about Japan.
One child put up her hand and said, "The Great Wall of China!"

(Ben Hewlett - The only full time professional Harmonica teacher in the UK!)

....

When asked to produce a slogan to encourage people to watch the film 'Amadeus,' Karl Hurcombe, at the time a Year 8 pupil at the Crypt School, wrote:

'It's thrilling
It's chilling
It's art.
No -
It's Mozart!'

I thought - and still think - this is brilliant!

(Philip Colls)

....

After a teacher had called out a pupil register at a fire drill outside the music block, one of my colleagues very dryly continued, "Bach...Beethoven...Mozart!"

....

The weekly class recorder sessions I used to give were both memorable and frustrating. Any commiserations?
The often excruciating sound didn't dampen my efforts and I soldiered on, in the interest of the children's musical education! It never ceased to amaze me how many different ways children came up with to get a sound out of the instrument. It was always tricky to keep everybody together - there was always someone who had gone on and found the work rather tedious - "I've done that already" or "I finished the book by myself, mummy says can I go on..." when most others found the lesson a weekly struggle (uphill!) We generally made progress and managed to produce a fairly musical sound by the end of term....!

(Rozanne Carpenter)

Taken from a school music project:
"Beethoven carried on composing, even though he went tone deaf."

(Rozanne Carpenter)

....

On a junior band course, a selection of music was being played, which had words to sing above the stave. In percussion music, the instructions for which beaters to use etc., is also written thus. All went well, all words correct and sung with gusto, when suddenly, twelve bars later, a small voice from the boy playing drum kit, beautifully performed a lesser known song: "Take brushes and tap single cymbal" - this led to a total collapse of the band!

....

One end of term concert, after many weeks of intense rehearsal, 'Finlandia' reached it's shattering final notes to tumultuous applause. Later, in the refreshment marquee, the parents of the timpanist came rushing up:
"It was wonderful", said mum, "it's the first time we've seen Robert play."
"Yes", said dad, "we were extremely impressed. It's taken us by complete surprise. We didn't know he could play so well!"
I offered modest words on progress, etc.
"Didn't his arms go up and down fast!" she gushed. "Gosh, I could even see the fluff flying off his little balls!"
She did, of course, mean the cotton and felt tipped (old and well used) timpani beaters, but, too late to stop the explosion of laughter for all in hearing distance!

(Clayton McCann)

....

As Head of a Junior Music School, I used to publish an information sheet for prospective students. I made the mistake of writing that tuition was given on a wide range of instruments, many of which could be initially loaned. The parent of a boy who had been learning the violin for ten weeks, wrote to complain that during that time, he had only ever studied the violin and wanted to know why he had not received lessons on any other instruments mentioned in my letter!

(Peter Barnes)

....

From a school music quiz:
What is a waltz?
Ans 1 - Is it a choice on a keyboard? *(Duncan)*
Ans 2 - It goes like this 123 123 123 123 123 123 123 123 123. *(Elizabeth)*

....

School and instrumental music

The children's thoughts

Music is a school subject where you might be able to learn to play an instrument. *(Luke)*

It's a fun lesson and you can learn about it easily! *(Alastair)*

...It's a unique lesson because it is the only lesson when you are allowed to make a lot of noise and it's called tuneful!
(Sarah)

Music is not really a lesson but it is more to do with dancing, rhythm, singing and having confidence. *(Lois)*

I hate music. It gives me a headache! *(Jack)*

....

Amusing incidents from the children

In the middle of orchestra, when we were playing 'Skip to my Loo,' somebody passed wind! *(Helena)*

When we were in our music lesson, Sir actually found out how to use a CD player. He had been trying to make it work since last term and all he had to do was press one button!
(Clare)

In our music lesson, Sir kept saying to us, "You're too loud, man!" We thought that was really funny! *(Jemma)*

I can never forget our first pop song we made up in Year 4. It was a failure called 'Elastic Band.'
It was some rubbish which went -
"Elastic Band isn't bigger than my hand.
Elastic Band - not brass - you can't lose hands in the grass!"
I feel so embarrassed when I think it was our best effort!
(Owen)

In our music lesson, Sir called David 'David Green, Sir' and Olivia a 'gasbag' because she was talking a lot! *(Joe)*

In my Year 6 music scholarship audition, I announced my double bass piece 'Scale insects.' The panel of judges all started laughing and the Director of Music ran out of the room and only came back a bit later after I had finished. He told me afterwards that I had said the title so quickly that it had sounded like something else! (Now I know what!) *(Izzy)*

I wanted to make a pop band at school and at our first practice, we had a huge argument and that was the first and last practice! *(Sam)*

We thought it was funny when our recorder teacher was playing 'Titanic' and she played the wrong note! We didn't think teachers did that. *(Robert)*

....

I had a recorder lesson and I put my recorder in my music bag and walked away. Then I came back and got my bag and went to my lesson. When I opened my bag, my hamster climbed out of it!

(Amy)

An amusing incident was in our music lesson when Sir was playing the piano, but we found out it wasn't him but a tape because there was a power cut and the machine stopped! *(Anon)*

When the class was singing 'I believe I can fly,' Michael fell off his chair! *(Tom)*

Nothing funny ever happens in our music lessons because our teacher is too serious and never has anything fun and is just boring... *(Anon)*

Everyone laughed when I came into class and pretended that my guitar was a gun! *(Jonathan)*

In windband, when everyone is playing well, sometimes somebody squeaks the clarinet part and everyone starts laughing! *(Lucy)*

Once, in my piano lesson, the children outside were making a lot of noise, so my teacher went to tell them off but when she tried to open the door, she pulled off the door handle! We stood there laughing as she tried to put it back. It took 5 minutes and by the time it was fixed, the noisy children had gone! *(Charlotte)*

When I first did the flute, I ran out of air and so I fell down and went all funny and then I got better. *(Marilyn)*

Nobody could sing in tune in our music lesson and we all think Sir listens to weird music! *(Michelle)*

My teacher sometimes gives me food in my piano lessons!
(David)

When I was playing my clarinet, I coughed and the right note came out! *(Nick)*

I wanted to learn the double bass and even the quarter size was bigger than me!

(Karis)

After a person came into class late, they said, "Sorry Sir, I was at windband." My teacher's response was, "I thought something smelt. Sit down!" *(Sheridan)*

I can't think of anything funny ever happening in a music lesson, but I can play the piano lying down on the piano stool! My teacher thought it was hysterical! *(James)*

Once in an orchestra, the conductor got very enthusiastic and his baton flew out of his hand and hit a second violin player on the head! *(Jennifer)*

....

"Classical music is ancient orchestral music." *(Sam)*

Thoughts and definitions of Classical music from the children...

It's old, well known music... *(Jamie)*

...produced a long time ago... *(Charles)*

...which has lasted for a long time and doesn't lose it's appeal!
(Andrew)

Well, Classical music is old-fashioned music, like Mozart.
(Dylan)

It's the opposite of pop... *(Sam)*

...because it doesn't have a strong beat. *(Jen)*

It's music with violins and stuff. It is NOT hip-hop! *(Jessica)*

Classical music is soft music, which just runs smoothly along, sometimes going back to the beginning again. *(Rosanna)*

It's not loud and was written long before Hammond keyboards and stereo symphonics... *(Andrew)*

...and you can play it without electricity! *(Noonie)*

So there are no electric instruments in Classical music. *(Harriett)*

It's non jazzy music. *(Anthony)*

It's so boring, but I have to put up with it because my dad likes it... *(Lindsay)*

Classical music is sort of sad music, I think. *(Charlotte)*

I don't like it because it's strange and you can't sing to it!
(Lauren)

It's old-fashioned music with lots of strings... *(Owen)*

...for the older generation. *(Sophie)*

My dad listens to Classical music really loudly, too loudly!
(Anon)

It's for old fogies who like to drink brandy! *(Hannah)*

People who are over 50 listen to Classical music. *(Georgie)*

It's boring granddad music! *(Patrick)*

"Romantic music is where the instruments fall in love!"
(Rebecca)
Thoughts and definitions of Romantic music from the children

Romantic music was composed in a certain period of time in history. *(Steph)*

It's quite old music, but more modern than Classical music. *(Elizabeth)*

It's slow, sweet, loving music... *(Hannah)*

...which has lots of feelings... *(Charlotte)*

...and is supposed to make you think of lovers! *(Tamsin)*

Romantic music is soppy for boys, nice for girls and some adults. It's anything with a red tenor or the word 'love' in the title! *(Owen)*

It's lovey dovey ... *(Mark)*

...kissy snoggy music!
(Rosie)

It has little cupids flying around shooting people! *(Francesca)*

It makes you feel all smoothey inside! *(Stephanie)*

It's stuff you turn on when your girlfriend comes round...
(Charles)

Boys buy romantic music to impress a girl, but it never works! *(Beth and Mandy)*

Romantic music is played in films when people fall in love!!! *(Hannah)*

...and love is in the air! *(Andrew)*

It's suited for love movies, like 'Romeo and Juliet.' *(Josh)*

Romantic music brings people together. *(Tom)*

It's for people who are in love. Are you, Sir? *(Emma)*

....

"An opera is a classical musical show." *(Runy)*

Thoughts and definitions about opera from the children

An opera is a group of people that do a play, but sing, instead of talk. *(Dylan)*

It's a long musical, with classical songs and a plot based mainly on gods or fat women! *(Owen)*

It is a story expressed in music. It is also very boring. *(Tim)*

In an opera, a person sings for hours and hours. *(Charlotte)*

There are very strong and very loud singers in it... *(John)*

...who have very big lungs... *(Anon)*

Opera is eardrum bursting music! *(Fergus)*

The singing is very high pitched and very low pitched. *(Abby)*

People who sing opera can break the windows! *(Stephanie)*

The people sing with their mouths wide open and make a loud noise. *(Samantha)*

The opera is where people sing like Pavarotti. *(Jean)*

The singers sing in a certain style, usually in a foreign language... *(Steven)*

...it's something which you can't understand. *(Ricky)*

Posh people go to the opera to make themselves look even more intelligent! *(Anon)*

....

Big, fat people sing opera!

(Lara)

"A string quartet is a string band." *(Jonathan)*

Thoughts and definitions about string quartets from the children

It is a selection of first and second violins, cellos and double basses and maybe a harp. It consists of 18-20 people. *(Gabrielle)*

A string quartet has 3 or 4 violins. *(Olly)*

It's a group of an orchestra who are all something to do with strings in one way or another... *(Max)*

A string quartet is an instrument with 4 strings. *(Matthew)*

What is a string quartet?
Ans.: "Hey? I've only been playing for 2 months!" *(Georgina)*

A string quartet? Is it a violin and stuff like that? *(Charlotte)*

....

A string quartet is where 4 people play string instruments like a mini orchestra.

(Charlotte)

"Bark and Handel were famous composers." *(Philip)*

Name some famous composers

Famous composers? Mozart and the Blood Hound Gang.
(Chris)

...Mozart, Beethoven, Handel and 'S Club 7' *(Nicky and Hannah)*

Some famous composers who have written instrumental and choral music are Bach, Beethoven and Motown. *(Karis)*

Bach, Paul MacCartney, Chopin, Brahms... *(Henry)*

Bach, Mozart, Beethoven and John Lennon. *(James)*

Mozart was a famous poser. *(Anon)*

....

"A symphony is a drum kit." *(Richard)*

Thoughts about instruments

A symphony is where all the instruments harmonise... *(Lara)*

Trumpets are amusing because they make the players faces go red! *(Emma)*

The double bass is basically the same size as the owner!
(Francesca)

The oboe sounds like a duck! *(Alicky)*

Stringed instruments are amusing because they make the sound with horse tails! *(Will)*

....

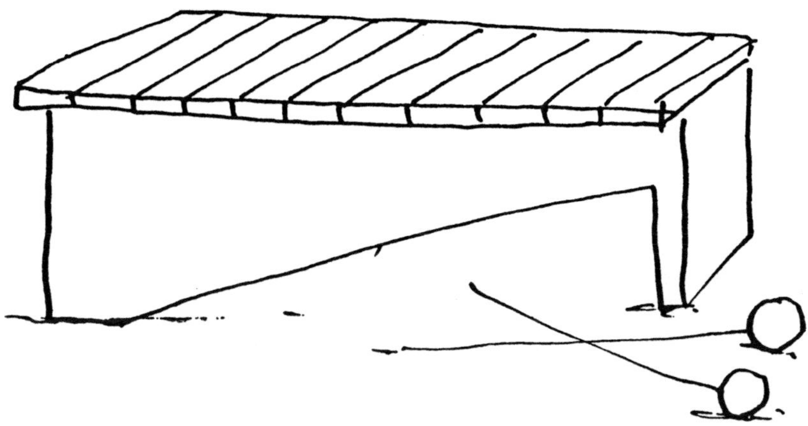

I think the xylophone is the funniest instrument, because all it really is, is bashing pieces of wood!

(Josh)

....

The four different groups of instruments in the orchestra are the strings, wood, brass and the rowdy section. *(Fergus)*

Strings, brass, woodwind and precision are the four groups of instruments in the orchestra. *(Anthony)*

The instruments in the orchestra are:
the windband, strings, percussion and brass. *(Harpreet)*

The French horn looks funny because it looks like it's all tied up in a knot! *(Steven)*

You don't really need to be talented to play the Tam Tam.
(Rhodri)

The lute is a funny looking instrument because it looks like a bent guitar! *(Jonathan)*

I think the tuba is a funny instrument because it's like my dad when he's eggy! *(Sam)*

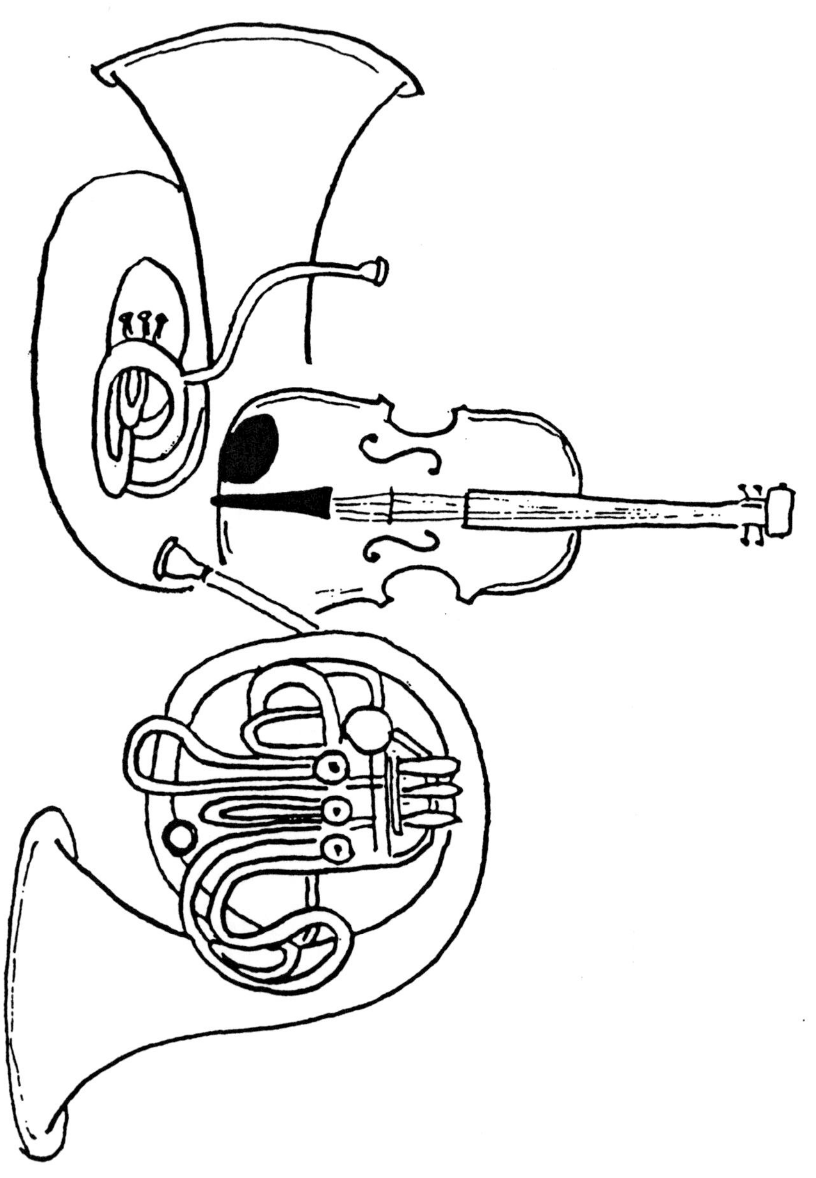

The tuba is a ridiculous sounding instrument! *(Olivia)*

Honky-tonks are funny instruments with a loony name.
(Owen)

....

"I would like to play the triple bass." *(Richard)*

Thoughts about playing instruments

Sometimes, I get the notes all mixed up and the tune goes all funny! *(Margot)*

Out of the piano and the glockenspiel, I prefer the piano because it's much more fun than trying to 'ting' the notes!
(Charlotte)

I like playing the saxophone, but I get eggy when I can't play a high D! *(Jasmine)*

I would like to play the drums because I like hitting things!
(Charlie)

I learn voice and piano and the favourite instrument is the one I carry round in my throat. *(Jemma)*

If I was to play an instrument, I would choose the drums so that I could annoy my mum, dad and sister! *(James)*

My favourite instrument is the sax because I think it's part of me and I love the sound. *(James)*

It's fun learning to play the piano - play famous tunes and you'll soon have an audience! (Owen)

....

My favourite instrument is the flute because my rat follows me round when I play it!

(Amy)

....

I would like to play the piano because it's simple and easy! *(Amy)*

I would like to play the drums because they are loud, like me!
(Anon)

If you bash a piano or randomly strum a guitar, you can pass for a musician. *(Owen)*

I used to play the sax, but it was too expensive... *(Jack)*

If I could play an instrument, I would choose the piano or the flute, because I like the sounds they make and also, people would think I was really clever! *(Lara)*

I can play really cool tunes on both the recorder and the piano! *(Owen)*

"An orchestra is a big classical music band." *(Tom)*

Thoughts about the orchestra

It's a band of mostly classical instrument players. *(Jake)*

It's a huge club where people play together. *(Sophie)*

The orchestra is like a choir, but it is made up of lots of musical instruments. *(Roland)*

The orchestra plays a lot of music all at once, but in an order so that it sounds nice! *(Amy)*

It is a group of people playing instruments that are in harmony with each other. *(Sabina)*

....

"He paints a musical picture." *(Daniel)*

Thoughts about the conductor from the children

The conductor pieces the orchestra together and gives the musicians something to do. *(Steven)*

He organises the orchestra... *(Courtney)*

...by telling the people in the orchestra to come in and out of the tune. *(Harriett)*

He controls the orchestra and orders them about! (Rosie)

He leads it, just like the leader of an army... *(Jade)*

...and acts like the boss! *(James)*

The conductor makes the people who play the instruments concentrate. *(Suzi)*

He reads the tune and then signals to the orchestra... *(Owen)*

...and makes sure the orchestra play the right notes! *(Alex)*

He stops and starts the instruments...*(Helen)*

...and waves his hands in time with the music. *(Claire)*

He helps the orchestra to be synchronised. *(Andrew)*

He has a baton and if he wants the orchestra to go high, he waves his baton high in the air. *(Laurence)*

He waves his stick around and bounces around a lot.
(Michael)

....

The conductor waves his fairy wand around.
(Alexander)

He points the stick at the orchestra so that they know when to play... *(Blaire)*

...and he keeps the instruments in time. *(Lindsay)*

Conductors wave a stick in the air and it makes the people playing the instruments play the right notes! *(Kathryn)*

The conductor waves his hands about to keep everyone in tune... *(Michelle)*

...and he lifts his hands to get louder and lowers them to get quieter. *(Ines)*

In our school, the conductors wave their arms around. They are supposed to keep us in time, but no one follows! *(Alicky)*

The conductor does nothing. I've been in an orchestra and everyone ignores him! *(Andy)*

....

"A stave is for balancing the notes on." *(Tom)*

What is a stave?

You plonk the notes on the stave. *(Heidi)*

The lines of the stave are for putting the notes on, to make the tune... *(Sophie)*

...it's easier to read the music if you use this! *(Jade)*

We use the stave so that we can tell the different notes apart.
(Caroline)

It's a note holder. It holds your notes in the right place.
(Georgina)

....

"A scale goes up and down like a yo-yo!" *(Izzy)*

What is a scale?

A scale is a bit of tough skin on a snake's back. *(Michael)*

It's something on a fish. *(Sophie)*

Is it a weight measurement? *(Lucy)*

You use them in Geography. *(Alex)*

It's something with 8 notes... *(Rosie)*

...which goes: du du du du du du du du... *(Amy)*

...or Do Re Me Fa So La Te Do... *(Elizabeth)*

...and you go 123123412312345... *(Charlotte)*

It's something you have to do to make a Grade. *(Sam)*

It's a piece of music that goes higher then lower... *(Kristian)*

...like a ladder of notes. *(Caroline)*

It's a little piece of music where you follow one note to the next... *(Alex)*

...it's easy! All you have to do is go up a note everytime! *(Laura)*

If you sing a scale, then you will know how high or how low your voice is! *(Udai)*

'Croquets,' 'redials' and 'sad faces'

Notation - alternative names!

♪ triplequaver (demisemiquaver!) *(Alex)*

♪ a double quaver (semiquaver) *(Anon)*

♪ those things you can eat! (quavers) *(Anon)*

....

♩ croquet *(Sian)* crocket *(Eleanor)* semicrotchet *(Nick)*

♩ mini *(Siobhan)* minibreve *(R.C.)* mininote *(R.C.)*

○ semibrief *(Lois)* semeybeat *(Adam)* semibreeze *(Bernard)*

....

Note values, expressed in fractions and decimal points! -

semibreve - 4/4
minim - 2/4
crotchet - 1/4
quaver - 0.5/4
semiquaver - 0.25/4
(Sabina)

....

𝄞 Tremble clef *(Sarah)* Treblebass *(Chris)*

𝄢 Brass clef *(Harpreet)*
Doublebass *(Chris)*
A sad face! (Text!) *(Phoebe)*

....

What is this sign? ♯ Ans. "Redial" *(Tom)*

Name these signs: ♯ sharp ♭ flat ♮ neutral *(Tim)*

Operatic pranks!

A singing teacher of considerable talent (and of a somewhat highly strung nature) had, by some misfortune of bad timetabling, found herself confronted by 70 pupils for a weekly singing lesson in the school hall, on the stage.

She spent a great deal of time teaching operatic choruses to the class, who usually displayed understandably minimal interest! On this particular day, unbeknown to her, a group of mischievous girls had hidden themselves below the stage, where the timpani were kept. She realised that about a third of the class were missing, but became impatient and proceeded to launch into warming up exercises for the operatic gymnastics which were to follow.

After the third exercise, a rather ominous boom emanated from beneath the stage and their classmates, primed to react, displayed the necessary exaggerated fear! The teacher went below to investigate, unsuccessfully, as the culprits merely hid themselves from view! After three such interruptions, her artistic temperament finally took over and she let fly exactly what she thought of the situation, hitting top C several times! Then, to the classes even greater amusement, she kicked the heater, (which was plugged into a recess on the stage floor) with such force, that it hurtled across the stage as far as the cord would allow. Somehow, the plug held in the socket and the force with which it had been propelled, simply brought it hurtling straight back at her!

The class then abandoned all pretence of straight faces and, unable to bear any more pranks, the teacher promptly gathered up her books and fled, in fury and outrage!

(Anon - one of those pupils!)

"A choir is lots of people...

Chapter 4

Choirs and concerts

...sinning together."

(Jennie)

The choir...

Children's thoughts

The choir is a musical group who don't use instruments, except for their voices. *(Jake)*

They sing in different octaves... *(Edward)*

...they sing in tune... *(Lloyd)*

...and they sing very nicely! *(Rosie)*

We were in choir and this boy had to sing on his own. He stood up and his flies were undone - he didn't know, but we could see his boxers! *(Caroline)*

In the choir, I didn't know the music, so I started to sing the wrong song which actually fitted the music! *(Robert)*

....

A choir is lots of people sinning together.

(Jennie)

We had been working towards our school prize-giving and things weren't going as well as I had hoped! During choir practice, a lot of fidgeting had been going on, so I threatened a bad mark if anyone moved during the songs. All was going well until Jessica fainted. Nobody moved and everyone kept singing and I looked straight ahead. At the end of the song, I stopped playing the piano and realised what had happened. I had been taken literally at my word!

(Rachael Sims)

....

Rehearsing a new setting of 'The Lord's Prayer', the choirmaster was very disappointed by the poor quality of sound. At the words 'Give us this day our daily bread,' he shouted out in exasperation, "Open your mouths!"

(Anon)

....

On a tour of Italy, our Prep School choir gave our first performance in Padua, with Thomas Tomkins' 'Preces and Responses.' Due to an unfortunate misunderstanding between the conductor and the only member of the choir who had perfect pitch, there were several false starts before, realising that we simply had to get on, the conductor encouraged us to continue, but we had to sing it a perfect 5th higher than usual!! We shrieked and strained all the way through, with smiles on our faces as if nothing was amiss! There were only a handful of people in the audience anyway and none of them were any the wiser!

(Rozanne Carpenter)

....

A few years ago, I, being the school's only pianist, was taking hymn practice for the whole primary school, alongside the Headteacher. We always did a double act! We usually tried to explain the meaning of some of the hymns and songs that we sang. We were, however, lost for words when, during the second verse of 'O Come all ye faithful' we came across the line, 'Lo, he abhors not the Virgin's womb!'

(Anon)

....

We were rehearsing for our annual Carol Service and the choir were on benches on a rostrum. We were singing through 'Hark the Herald angels sing' and as we sang the last line of the chorus, the whole back row fell off the benches backwards and all that could be seen were pairs of legs!

(Rachael Sims)

I was playing the piano for some auditions for the show 'Rose Marie' by Rudolf Friml. One of the audition pieces was 'When I'm calling you' which has in it, a phrase written - 'When I'm calling you.....oo.....oo' because of the length of the melody on the word 'you.' One naive soprano sang "When I'm calling you, double O, double O." She didn't get the part!

....

I play the piano for the local choral society and in rehearsals, the piano is positioned very near to the alto section - the altos are usually the ones who talk most while the conductor is rehearsing the other parts. In an effort to get a point across one week, I interrupted the conductor with the remark, "Do you mind, I can't hear what the altos are talking about!"

(Anon)

....

Concerts

Amusing incidents

When I was in a concert, I said what I was going to play and then I played something else, but I don't think anybody noticed! *(Samuel)*

We couldn't stop laughing at a concert when someone's drumstick went flying into the audience. He had been playing well until then! *(Jamie and Runy)*

The drums collapsed when the drummer was playing. We all thought it was very funny, but he didn't! *(Callum)*

In Swing Band, everyone was playing and we were coming up to a sax solo, but suddenly there was silence and nobody played it! *(Harry)*

....

Orchestral playing renders a whole new meaning to the word 'unison!'

(Anon)

At a school concert, the orchestra was playing an easy arrangement of the 'James Bond' theme and I was not able to reach down to play the last note on my bassoon because it's still rather big for me! So the conductor got one of my friends to sit next to me and she had to cover the correct holes to make the last note sound! The audience thought this was very funny and we got a special clap from them!

(Suzi)

....

I played the cello in a local orchestra and one Saturday morning, we rehearsed Tchaikowski's Pathetique Symphony. The second movement (in 5/4 time) was the most interesting, as the conductor had his own method of coping with the rhythm. He conducted 4 beats the normal way and then stuck out his elbow for the 5th beat!

(Anon)

....

I was in the audience of a concert being given by a local youth orchestra. This is a true conversation that I heard:
Lady to her friend: "I wonder why some string players have new shiny instruments?"
Her friend replied: "The orchestra can't afford to buy all new instruments. It must be 'first come, first served,' with those arriving early enough having the chance to get the new shiny ones!"

(Peter Barnes)

....

Six year old at the end of a rehearsal: "I didn't drop my violin once today, did I?"

(Elizabeth Dwinnell)

....

Just prior to playing a solo in her first concert, an enthusiastic pupil said to me, "I washed my clarinet ready for the concert!" She had put the whole thing into a bowl of washing up liquid!

(Lynne Sharratt)

A violinist to a conductor of a village orchestra, when asked to tune up, said, "I don't like my strings too tight!"

....

When asked to re-tune, a second violinist indignantly replied "But I tuned up last week!"

(S.M. Murphy)

....

At a most memorable informal concert, a young boy, aged about 8, climbed onto the piano stool and stretched to put his music on the music desk of the school Bechstein grand. There was to be no piano concerto, but a short piece in the five finger hand position. The boy looked confident and the audience hushed. He started confidently, but after a few notes, the music ground to a halt. Undeterred, he duly started again. A look of 'well it goes right at home' appeared on his face when the music ground to a halt at the same place. Very quickly, the Director of Music rushed to the piano to sort out the problem. He looked at the music and then at the boy and told him not to move. The piano was moved three inches to the right and the performer was told to start again. A successful playing then ensued to rapturous applause at the end!

(David Crabtree)

At a concert at my daughter's school, the dining hall was being used for the orchestra to perform and entertain parents before a fireworks display.

Whilst the orchestra was in full swing, the conductor's face, contorted with concentration, suddenly gave way to a look of total disbelief. A kitchen door swung open and out came a dinner lady, laden with crockery, heading straight for the canteen, which wasn't actually being used that night.
She walked around the orchestra, pushed herself quite confidently through the brass section, the children all hastily moving out of her way to clear an impromptu path, one hand clutching their instruments, the other frantically trying to steady their stands and chairs and yet somehow still managing to keep going!

She went straight to the back of the orchestra. The timps had to be squeezed passed and a music teacher had to move very rapidly to avoid a head-on collision with his keyboard! She did whatever she had intended to do at the canteen and then proceeded to return the way she had come, disappearing into the kitchen, quite oblivious of the havoc she'd caused!

The children were both astonished and amused, but, as instructed, kept going to the end of the piece! It was a most entertaining performance!

(Rozanne Carpenter)

....

POP! Pain Or Pleasure?! (Anon)

Pop music is poptastic! (Zak)

It evolved in the '90's for young people. (Matthew)

It's the up-to-date 'now' music! (Shane)

...it's electric music... (Charlotte)

...it's groovy...(Lois)

*...and funky stuff that most teenagers love to listen to...
(Harriett)*

...and it's better than opera! (Lily)

*It's fairly loud dance music, which makes a lot of money by
being sung by men and women in sexy costumes. (Simon)*

....

*Pop music is NOT classical - just the opposite! (Nicky and
Hannah)*

*It's performed by a band on modern instruments and
NOT by an orchestra. (Jo)*

*It's where young people jump up and down and sing songs
in a hippy way. (Victoria)*

People with funny hair play guitar in pop music! (Edward)

....

Pop is upbeat lively music which is easy to pick up. (Abigail)

It's a racket... (Rebecca)

...fast and energetic... (Helena)

...wild music! (Jessica)

Good pop songs have a boppy beat... (Tom)

...with a modern day tune. (Ella)

The tune has to have a bit of 'go' in it! (Amy)

Pop has cool words and a cool beat. (Emily)

*It HAS to have a good tune, or I'll refuse to listen to it!
(Aniela)*

It makes you go pop and makes people go mad! (Colomo)

*It's the best thing ever. I couldn't live without my S Club 7
CD and my CD player! (Anita)*

*Unlike some others, S Club 7 actually has tunes and
patterns! (Rosie)*

*I think it's an evil creation designed to shock the innocent
music lover! (Owen)*

....

Coda

I love music because it rules! (Charles)

It makes you feel good! (James)

Life would be dull without it! (Alexander)

How can anyone not like it?! (Heather)

Music is wicked, fun and can overcome nerves. (Izzy)

It's part of my life. (Harriet)

*There's something about it that makes you want to take part.
(Charlie)*

*If there was no music, there wouldn't be any CDs or tapes,
so I like music! (Ollie)*

*It's remarkable the way a person and an instrument combine
lovingly, like a mother and child! (Elizabeth)*

Everyone has music in their soul. (Anon)

It's the best thing in the world... (Stacey)

...and the world just wouldn't be without it! (Charlotte)

Music is magical! (Sophie)

I LOVE MUSIC - ANYTIME, ANYWHERE! (ANIELA)

....

Printed in the United Kingdom
by Lightning Source UK Ltd.
124562UK00001B/202/A